ASHA

ISBN-13: 978-1544241920

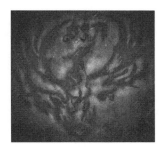

COPYRIGHT ©2016 {WINSTON HEAD}

ALL RIGHTS RESERVED

Realize you are from Good Spirit, made of Good Spirit, and will return to Good Spirit. When you understand this your vibration rises. You become a mighty spiritual force creating in the plastic medium of energy.

I AM GOD'S THOUGHT. I LIVE IN GOD'S IDEA; PERFECTION.

The whole universe vibrates with expectant energy, for God is with child (creative thought). All throughout the celestial palace the prospect of ever expanding good radiates brilliant and bright with joy as the highest principle of good shines the light of observance on the dark waves; that is the plastic medium of creation. In conformity to law, the wise Lord's highest desire was focused into form; young, timeless, and beneficial to all.

KNOW ONLY GOOD.

Perceive and understand only the good and let your experience and practice be the same.
Be aware at all times of your high standing. Always remember the covenant written on your mind, that you might not forget you are a child of the King.

I HAVE THE MIND OF CHRIST.

MY ONLY JOB IS TO ALIGN WITH, AND HOLD CONTINUOUSLY IN MIND THE ATTRIBUTES OF GOD. LOVE, LIFE, PEACE, JOY, POWER, AND FREEDOM; AND BE THOSE ATTRIBUTES. MY MIND IS GOD, MY THOUGHTS ARE NOT ALWAYS GOD; MAY MY THOUGHTS ALIGN WITH MIND.

CREATE WITH WORD.

These four powers are the mental power concerned with forming. Temperance – self restraint, do not sin or think error.
Fortitude - strength in facing adversity without fear; without doubt. Reason – a basis or a cause for a belief, the highest truth, Asha. Energy – a source of usable power, God the highest principle of good.

BELIEVE ONLY THE HIGHEST TRUTH AND ENTER ASHA.

As the Wise Lord is perfect, so His idea of creation is perfect, this is called Asha (truth). This idea of truth is the very spirit of God. It is much more than not making a false statement, it is the true vision of God's ideal existence. It is the real above all real, the highest truth; creation in perfect harmony where nothing occurs at the expense or harm of another.

I LOOK INWARD TO THE GOD MIND AND I SEE TRUTH, AND EXPERIENCE SOUNDNESS OF MIND.

THOUGHTS MAKE YOUR WORLD, BELIEFS MAKE YOUR THOUGHTS, REASON MAKES YOUR BELIEFS. MIND REASONS, MIND IS THE REASON. KNOW THIS, THEN ILLUSION GOES AWAY. BELIEF IN ONLY GOOD; IT IS THIS COMPLETE TRUST THAT BRINGS OUT MANIFESTATIONS NOW, REAL AS THEY ALREADY ARE, BY MEANS OF REASON.

RESONANCE: I KNOW BEING GRATEFUL WILL BRING MORE THINGS TO BE GRATEFUL FOR.

I AM GRATEFUL FOR LIFE.
I AM GRATEFUL FOR LOVE.
I AM GRATEFUL FOR FAMILY.
I AM GRATEFUL FOR FRIENDS.
I AM GRATEFUL FOR PROTECTION.
I AM GRATEFUL FOR PROVISION.
I AM GRATEFUL FOR PEACE.
I AM GRATEFUL FOR JOY.

I AM GRATEFUL FOR I LIVE IN THIS, I LIVE IN GOD MY GOOD.

I WILL SEEK FIRST THE THOUGHT OF GOD. ASHA.

THE PERFECT CREATOR'S PERFECT MIND CREATED A PERFECT THOUGHT. I AM THAT THOUGHT. I AM PERFECT SPIRIT. I CHOOSE NOT TO BE DOUBLE MINDED, I CHOOSE TO THINK GOD NOT THE LIE. I AM PERFECT SPIRIT GOD'S CHILD (THOUGHT) AND SPIRIT MAKES BODY (FORM), THEREFORE MY BODY IS PERFECT; MY WORLD IS PERFECT.

ON A SUBCONSCIOUS LEVEL I LIVE IN TRUTH AND THE LIE OF DISCORD DISAPPEARS; THE SPELL OF SEPARATION IS BROKEN.
IN TRUTH ALL IS GOOD; ALL IS GOD.

I AM AWAKENED
TO WHO I AM.

I have shed the illusion of the lower animal; I have let go all error. I refuse to hold the vibrations, feelings, or emotions of the lie. I live only in the vibration of truth (Asha) God's highest idea of good. My eyes will not see nor ears hear the lie and illusion.

I turn away if I sense bad energy. I turn away and remove myself if others choose bad energy. No one can force bad energy on me for I am light and in light there is no darkness. This opinion or thought I hold is the key to the kingdom and this wisdom rules both worlds.

I WILL ASK MYSELF A QUESTION NOT CONCERNED WITH HOW I WANT OTHERS TO PERCEIVE ME, OR AN IMAGE TO PROJECT, BUT AN HONEST QUESTION LOOKING FOR AN HONEST ANSWER.

What Energy Am I Really?

There are two kinds of contraries. One whose differences are of function such as hot and cold, high and low, light and heavy, and full and empty which work together in harmony. Then there are contraries of substance which cannot combine such as good and evil, love and hate, health and sickness, truth and lie, and life and death.

FOR WHEN THE TRUTH IS TOLD
THE LIE IS EXPOSED FOR WHAT IT
IS, NOTHING. WHERE HEALTH IS,
SICKNESS IS NOT TO BE FOUND.
IT'S LIKE TURNING ON A LIGHT IN
A DARK ROOM, THERE IS NO BIG
FIGHT, THE LIGHT JUST FILLS THE
ROOM AND DARKNESS IS GONE.

SO ASK YOURSELF:
WHAT ENERGY AM I?

AM I LOVE OR HATE?

DO I BRING PEACE OR DISCORD?

DO I HOLD JOY OR
TROUBLE?

AM I FEARFUL AND DOUBTING?

Take an honest look inside is your energy good or evil. The energy of the seed of a tree will produce a tree. The energy of the seed of an animal will produce an animal. The energy of the seed of the good mind will produce good. The energy of the seed of the evil energy will produce evil.

So again ask yourself what energy am I really? What vibration, feeling emotion do I hold? That's what will manifest in your world that's the consciousness you will take to the next world.

So find God (the highest principle of good) now. Be love, peace, joy, now.

Today is the day of salvation, envelope yourself in God's idea, I am love, I am life, I am peace, I am joy, I am one with God, and evil cannot enter me.

Live consciously, good thoughts, good words, good deeds.

I WILL RELEASE MY OWN IDEAS TO RECEIVE GOD'S IDEA.

Removing the corruption puts potentialities to their proper use. You must burn out the impurities to find the true essence. Purity is a must, if your vessel is mixed with poison pour it out and fill it with pure substance. It takes a long time to purify a vessel one drop at a time, that in my opinion is too much trust in time. Trust God pour out your vessel and let God fill it with Himself.

THERE IS NOTHING
FOR ME OUTSIDE .

I have spent too long looking outside myself, looking for meaning, purpose, affirmation, approval, love, truth, happiness, and God. Just to find myself ever searching. So I quiet all the many thoughts and ideas and stories. And I go inside and there I see Jesus. And I realize there is no separation from my good my God. We are one, all the truth, happiness I was looking for is here now. I am that, I am, and now that I know this, it is, good is, God is.

GOOD IS GOOD.
BAD IS BAD.

The original word of the good religion is that all good comes from the Creator and that no evil comes from him. From this original word is the spiritual world made straight and the material world brought into order. The original word of false religion is that evil comes from the Creator. In this false idea is all the evil that creatures suffer.

I AM IN I AM.

I LIVE IN GOD. GOD IS GOOD.
GOD IS OMNIPRESENT. THAT
MEANS MY GOOD IS
OMNIPRESENT.

MY GOD IS HERE NOW, MY GOOD IS
HERE NOW.

TELL THE TRUTH.

Giving true witness a man will be saved. Only think and speak truth to yourself and it will form. Think God's highest idea of truth (Asha) and live. Keep the power of truth in mind and make it your model. Then trust God and let it be because it is, and you will see it already is. Don't worry or strive to make something happen, don't try and force it, just align.

EVERYONE WHO IS
OF THE TRUTH
HEARS THE TRUTH.

When man sins or thinks, speaks or acts in error it is against his nature, for he comes from the Good Spirit, and will return to the Good Spirit.

God put the good mind or divine spark in all his creatures so it has a guide at all times. It's how the seed knows to climb out of the ground and become a plant, how the planets stay there course, and how man will find his way home to Asha (truth).

LIVING IN TRUTH IS LIFE WITHOUT ENEMIES FOR EVIL, THE LIE, AND ILLUSION IS RENDERED NOTHING. SO GO ASHAVAN (TRUTH KNOWER) IN TRUTH AND ENJOY THIS WONDERFUL LIFE, KNOWING YOU ARE GOD'S THOUGHT LIVING IN GOD'S IDEA, PERFECTION.

Made in the USA
Monee, IL
03 May 2023

32928207R00025